KU-361-708

FUN WITH
THE CELTS
and
THE VIKINGS

DEADLY! IRISH HISTORY – THE VIKINGS

'madcap, marauding, entertaining and highly informative ... all proving that Irish history isn't boring at all ... it's deadly!'

Fallen Star Stories

DEADLY! IRISH HISTORY – THE CELTS

'accessible, anarchic and crammed with cartoons and wacky illustrations, this book is as deadly as Irish history gets!'

RTÉ Guide

'Farrelly's writing and drawings never miss a beat in this well-informed and witty account of the Celts ... Great fun!'

Children's Books Ireland

WORLD BOOK DAY

World Book Day's mission is to offer every child and young person the opportunity to read and love books by giving you the chance to have a book of your own.

To find out more, and for loads of fun activities and recommendations to help you keep reading visit **worldbookday.com**

World Book Day is a charity funded by publishers and booksellers in the UK and Ireland.

World Book Day is also made possible by generous sponsorship from National Book Tokens and support from authors and illustrators.

John Farrelly was born and raised in a village just outside Newry, County Down. He wouldn't say his family home was small but the front and back door was the same. He enjoyed school and thinks the education system in Irelandia is the bestest. After dropping out of art college, he worked in an amusement park. He was fired but he took them for funfair dismissal. Then he became a freelance caricature artist. It's a very secure job — no one else wants it. The O'Brien Press stupidly let him write and illustrate the first book in the **Deadly! Irish History** series about **THE VIKINGS** and now they can't get rid of him. He went on to write and illustrate his second book in the series on **THE CELTS**. And he didn't stop there. Next up are **THE NORMANS**, with their castles and all the shenanigans of medieval life. This World Book Day book is just some of the fun stuff you can find in his books.

DEADLY!
IRISH HISTORY

FUN WITH

THE CELTS

and

THE VIKINGS

Written and Illustrated by
JOHN FARRELLY

THE O'BRIEN PRESS
DUBLIN

First published 2022 by
The O'Brien Press Ltd,
12 Terenure Road East, Rathgar,
Dublin 6, D06 HD27 Ireland.
Tel: +353 1 4923333; Fax: +353 1 4922777
E-mail: books@obrien.ie
Website: obrien.ie
The O'Brien Press is a member of Publishing Ireland

ISBN: 978-1-78849-315-4

1 3 5 7 8 6 4 2
22 24 23

Cover artwork by John Farrelly, design by Emma Byrne
Internal design by Bex Sheridan and Brendan O'Reilly
Printed in the UK by Clays Ltd, Elcograf S.p.A.
The paper in this book is produced using pulp from managed forests.

Published in

DUBLIN

UNESCO
City of Literature

CONTENTS

WHO WERE THE CELTS?

The word *Celt* comes from the Greek word *Keltoi*, the name the Greeks called a group of people living in Europe nearly three thousand years ago. What Keltoi means we don't know, but the Celts were feared and respected by their enemies. At one time, the Celts were the most powerful people in central Europe and there were loads of Celtic tribes, who spoke a similar language. They spread outwards across Europe, making their way to France, Britain and Ireland. It's not known exactly how and when the Celts came to Ireland, but it is thought they began arriving around 700–600 BCE. Later Celtic settlers brought with them a new metal called iron, which replaced the weaker metal bronze. This is what historians call the Iron Age.

The Celts were very successful in establishing themselves in Ireland, which they did over a long period of time, not all at once. Some Celtic tribes lived peacefully alongside the native Irish, while others took what they wanted by force. Eventually, they became more or less one people, and though some historians don't like the use of the word 'Celtic', it has come to be used in a general way to describe the people, culture and art in Ireland from 700 BCE to the arrival of Christianity in the early 5th century.

Irish Celts took on a flavour of their own – they were different in lots of ways from the other Celtic tribes living in Europe and even across the Irish Sea in Britain. Even after Saint Patrick arrived on Irish soil, many pagan Celtic practices stayed the same for centuries, and Ireland still considers itself a Celtic country.

Roundhouses lasted about 10 years and were home to about 12-14 people. Smaller animals were taken into the house at night for warmth and protection. Geese acted as guard dogs. They had great eyesight, were very noisy and territorial and couldn't be bribed with meat like dogs could.

Meat and fish hanging in smoke for preservation

Thatch of river reed and hazel

Two woven willow wattle walls with straw filling and the outside covered in daub (mix of mud, straw and dung)

DEADLY MEDLEY!

Can you find these things?

☐ Goat and sheepskins (hint: on floor)

☐ Cauldrons

☐ Fidchell board game

☐ Leather tanning frame

☐ Child minding the fire

☐ Slave gathering dung for manure and daub

☐ Goose guard 'dog'

☐ Animal pens

☐ Oven

☐ Quern (hint: two stones that were used for grinding corn)

☐ Butter churn

Answers on pages 26–7

DEADLY! CRAFTY — A ROUNDHOUSE

1) To make the roof, draw a circle on a piece of thin card. You can use a compass, or if you want a bigger house, use a pencil tied to a piece of string and, with the other end fixed down, draw out a big circle.

2) Draw a line from the middle of the circle to the edge, then draw another one at an angle to the first. The smaller the gap between your two lines, the steeper the roof will be. A right angle or slightly less is best.

3) Cut out the circle and along both lines.

4) Overlap the ends to form a cone. Tape or glue the overlap.

5) To make thatch, glue straw or strips of yellow paper onto the roof. Or just draw it on with a yellow marker.

6) For the walls, measure the diameter of the bottom of the roof and cut a strip of card three times that length. (If the diameter is 15 cm, the strip will need to be 40–45 cm.)

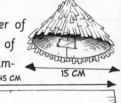

45 CM

15 CM

7) Cut the strip to roughly the same height as your roof. Cut a slot for the door, but don't cut all the way to the top.

8) Paint the card brown and add some lines for a wattle and daub effect. Or paint the card grey and draw on a stone effect. Stick the ends together.

9) To make a base, use green card or card painted green. Add some lines for a grass effect, and even some flowers.

DEADLY! CRAFTY INSULT GENERATOR

When in combat, you have to fight not only with your weapons, but also your tongue! Irish Celt warriors taunted and insulted their enemies before, during and after a battle, a bit like how boxers and MMA fighters trash-talk each other today.

This was an art in itself. It wasn't just a matter of saying, 'You smell bad', you had to use a bit of imagination. To get you started, pick one phrase from each column and mix them up to make some great insults and taunts that will make your foes run crying to mammy.

	A	B	C	
Your	mother	has a face like	burnt thatch	
	sister	loves to eat	week-old milk	
	father	wears	a baby's nappy	
	brother	has a head like	cold porridge	*and*
you	sick	squirrel	with two broken legs	
fight	dead	chicken	with the pox	
like a	blind	sheep	with no head	
	drowned	duck	with a smelly bottom	*and*
Your	sword	is only fit for	a pretendy fight!	
	spear	is only good for	a baby's toy!	
	chariot	is only useful for	the dung heap!	

ROUNDHOUSERS
A CELTIC SOAP OPERA

Over the centuries, loads of stuff from the Celtic era has been discovered in Ireland. Some of it was found in bogs, which preserved it, and some of it was buried treasure hoards. Other things were found in graves with their owners. Most of it ended up in museums. See if you can find these things in this episode of *Roundhousers*. **Answers on page 28.**

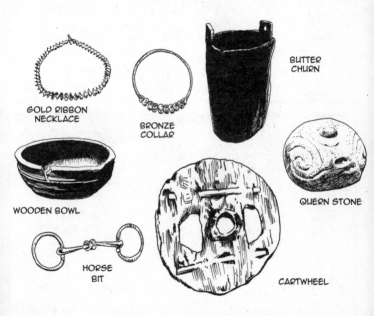

GOLD RIBBON NECKLACE

BRONZE COLLAR

BUTTER CHURN

WOODEN BOWL

QUERN STONE

HORSE BIT

CARTWHEEL

SCABBARD

SWORD HILT

FEASTING CUP

TANKARD

BROOCH

BRONZE DISC

BRONZE BOWL

17

19

20

23

DID YOU FIND ALL THE OBJECTS FROM THE MUSEUMS? ANSWERS ON PAGE 28.

NEXT TIME ON

Roundhousers

KING CONALL MESSES UP A CATTLE-RAID AND GRÁINNE GETS A NEW FOSTER-BROTHER.

TIMELINE

700–600 BCE – Celts begin arriving in Ireland towards the end of the Bronze Age.

500 BCE – The Iron Age in Ireland begins.

390–200 BCE – The Clonycavan man is sacrificed around this time. His body is found preserved in a bog early in the 21st Century.

200 BCE – Carvings on the Turoe Stone, Co. Galway, show European La Tène influence.

100 BCE – The Celts build a series of roads called slite throughout Ireland.

95 BCE – A great temple is built – and destroyed – at Eamhain Mhacha.

43 BCE – Pomponius Mela writes about how Ireland is rich with grassland and exploding cattle.

35 BCE – Diodorus Siculus writes in his Historical Library that the Irish eat human flesh. Was he fibbing or was Ireland full of ZOMBIES?!

AD 82 – Roman general Gnaeus Julius Agricola considers conquering Ireland but returns to Rome where he dies of food poisoning.

AD 140 – Greek map-maker Claudius Ptolemy makes the first known map of Ireland.

AD 400 – Niall Noigiallach (Niall of the Nine Hostages) rules Ireland.

AD 403 – A 16-year-old boy named Maewyn Succat is kidnapped by Irish raiders from his home in Britain and sold into slavery. He later escapes, becomes a bishop and calls himself Patrick.

AD 432 – Saint Patrick arrives, bringing Christianity to Ireland. The Celtic age ends.

All dates are approximate.

ANSWERS TO INSIDE A ROUNDHOUSE

1) Goat and sheepskins
2) Cauldrons
3) Fidchell board game
4) Leather tanning frame
5) Child minding the fire
6) Slave gathering dung for manure and daub
7) Goose guard 'dog'
8) Animal pens
9) Oven
10) Quern
11) Butter churn

ANSWERS TO ROUNDHOUSERS

GOLD RIBBON NECKLACE PAGE 17

BRONZE COLLAR PAGE 17

WOODEN BOWL PAGE 17

BUTTER CHURN PAGE 17

QUERN STONE PAGE 18

HORSE BIT PAGE 19

CARTWHEEL PAGE 19

SWORD HILT & SCABBARD PAGE 20

BROOCH PAGE 21

FEASTING CUP & TANKARD PAGE 21

BRONZE DISC PAGE 21

BRONZE BOWL PAGE 23

SO WHO WERE THESE VIKINGS, THEN?

Well, for a start *viking* was something they did, not something they were. They called themselves *Norraener Menn* or Norse Men, and the first wave of Vikings came from Norway. The Irish sometimes called them *Lochlannaigh*, 'men from the land of lakes'. The monks whose monasteries they raided in the 9th century called them 'pagans' or 'heathens'. To go 'a-viking' meant to go off on a boat somewhere in search of gold and adventure, and the Vikings were very good at viking, so the name stuck. These warriors from the cold north earned a fearsome reputation for killing, looting and pillaging.

They were feared so much that one Irish monk wrote a poem being thankful for a wet and windy night as Vikings only ever came when the seas were calm.

Fierce is the wind tonight,
It tosses the sea's white mane;
I need not fear the violent
warriors from Norway
Crossing the Irish Sea.

If newspapers had been around back then, we may have seen headlines like these about them:

Ye Olden Times

AD 795

IRISH MONASTERY RAIDED BY VIKINGS

DOZENS KILLED

The surviving members of a sleepy island community of monks were left traumatised after a lightning raid by foreign savages earlier today.

Dozens of monks were murdered while others were beaten or taken prisoner at the monastic settlement on Rechru Island, just off the coast of

Rechru Island

WEATHER
Look at your window, dearie!

Past Times

A.D. 798   1 GROAT

PILLAGE IDIOTS!
VIKINGS AT IT AGAIN!

YESTERDAY'S NEWS

VIKING PLUNDER WONDER!
Connacht attacked   AD 807

Then again, the Vikings were no more savage than other people throughout history ...

WORLD 🌐 NEWS

AD1221

GENGHIS KHAN MURDERS 40 MILLION PEOPLE

"If anybody can, Genghis Khan," says aide.

THE MOON

AD1462

Competition to give Vlad a nickname on page 5!

VLAD IMPALES 100,000

Bad Lad Vlad Tad Mad

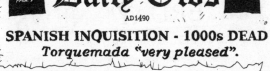

HOROSCOPES PAGE 9

Daily Olds

BINGO PAGE 12

AD1490

SPANISH INQUISITION - 1000s DEAD
Torquemada "very pleased".

Say hello to Snorri the Fib-Teller. Sometimes he's a wee bit economical with the truth. Which of his statements do you think are true? **Answers below.**

A) A VIKING LONGSHIP CAN TRAVEL 100 KM IN ONE DAY.

B) A VIKING SHIP IS AS LONG AS THE PITCH AT CROKE PARK.

C) IT TAKES 70 TREES TO BUILD A LONGSHIP.

D) IT TAKES THE WOOL OF 500 SHEEP TO MAKE THE SAIL FOR A LONGSHIP.

E) THE MAST ON A LONGSHIP IS 25 M TALL.

ANSWERS: Snorri is a right liar. **ALL** those statements are false. a) A Viking longship could travel 190 km in a single day. b) A typical longship was 30 m in length, so Croke Park is about 5 ships long and 3 ships wide. c) It took 91 oak, willow, pine and ash trees, to make one ship. d) It took the wool from 1,000 sheep to make the sail. That's a lot of naked sheep! e) The mast on a typical Viking ship was 16 m tall.

THE LONGSHIP

Although the first longships that brought the Vikings to Ireland were built in Norway, a ship similar to the one on the next few pages was found sunk in a harbour in Denmark that was made from oak trees possibly felled in Glendalough, Co. Wicklow in the year 1042. This means that the Vikings must have built longships in Ireland after they settled there.

After all the food and water supplies were loaded, as well as shields and weapons, it was a pretty tight squeeze aboard the ship. As they couldn't very well light a fire to cook food aboard a wooden ship, the men brought dried meat and fish, as well as barrels of sour milk (YUCK!) and fresh water. Just in case they were close enough to shore to be able to light a fire and cook something hot, like a nice mutton stew, they also took a cauldron – a big cooking pot.

A WEEK OR MORE TO GET THERE ...

... A WEEK OR MORE TO GET BACK.

NORWAY

The voyage between Norway and Ireland took at least a week and sometimes much longer, so they had to bring enough supplies for the journey there and back.

Each man had a sea-chest to keep his stuff safe and he sat on this when the ship had to be rowed. Can you tell what these belongings are just from their silhouettes? Answers below.

1.

The helmsman kept the ship on course using the steering-oar.

2.

3.

4.

Even hardy sailors could get sea-sick sometimes!

ANSWERS: 1) Helmet. Whether it's made of leather or iron, never go anywhere without your helmet. 2) Knife. Vikings used these for whittling wood but could be useful in close combat! 3) Drinking horn. Made from cow or goat horn, this couldn't be put down when it was full so you had to drink the lot in one go. 4) Thor's hammer amulet. Sailors wore this for protection. (More lore about Thor you will adore late-or.)

Although the ship was nearly watertight, plenty of buckets and scoops were kept onboard to bail out bilge water when the sea got rough – which was often! If there weren't enough buckets, they used their helmets.

No he's not taking a selfie. Vikings may have used a 'sunstone' to navigate when it got cloudy. And the seas around Ireland were always cloudy! Other ways they navigated were by the stars and watching for birds that flew near land.

The Vikings carved ugly figureheads to scare away the evil gods of the sea and to terrify their enemies. Maybe they used your older brother or sister as a model! Sometimes these were dragon heads.

This made many people call the longboats 'dragon ships', which does sound pretty cool!

INSIDE AN IRISH VIKING HOUSE

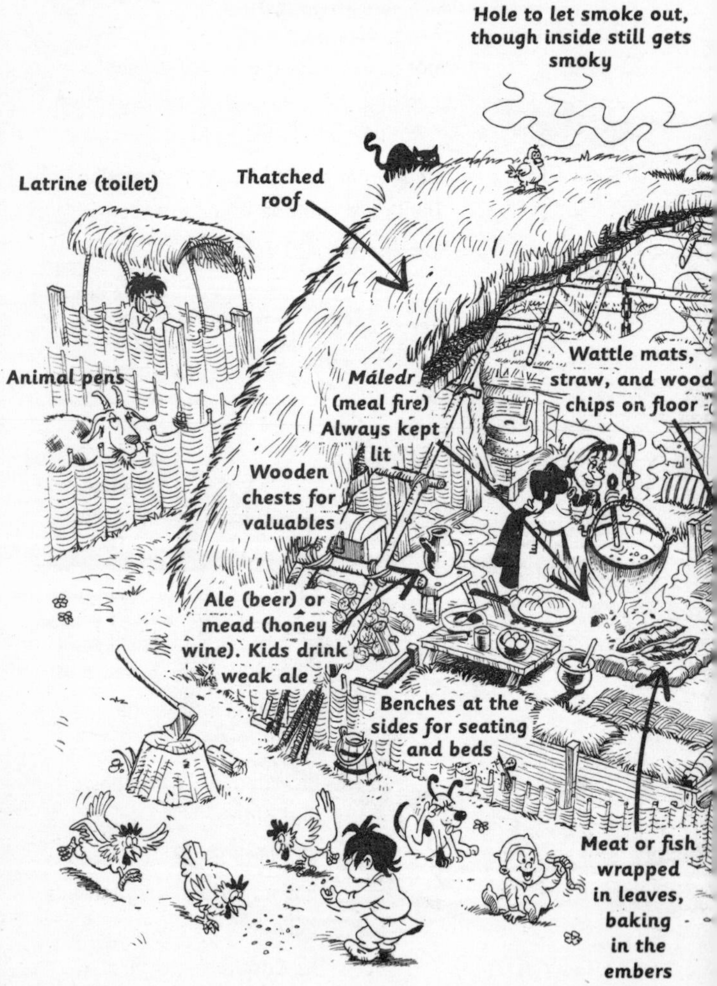

Hole to let smoke out, though inside still gets smoky

Latrine (toilet)

Thatched roof

Animal pens

Wattle mats, straw, and wood chips on floor

Máledr (meal fire) Always kept lit

Wooden chests for valuables

Ale (beer) or mead (honey wine). Kids drink weak ale

Benches at the sides for seating and beds

Meat or fish wrapped in leaves, baking in the embers

DEADLY! MEDLEY

Can you find these things?

☐ Weaving loom. Wool comes from the family's sheep. Clothes, blankets, tapestries and even ships' sails are made on the loom.

☐ An iron (made from heated glass) for pressing clothes. The board is made from whalebone.

☐ Tallow (animal fat) candles

☐ Tapestries to decorate the walls and keep heat in

☐ Weapon and shield display on wall

☐ Clay jugs and jars, all imported

☐ Soapstone bowl

☐ Quern-stone for grinding grain to make bread

☐ Rye or barley bread baking on skillets

☐ Iron or soapstone cooking pot

☐ Wooden bucket, bowl and plate.

☐ Metal knives and spoons but no forks – they haven't been invented yet!

☐ Cushions and furs

No
~~dows~~

~~od in~~
~~acks~~

~~Vattle~~
~~walls~~

ANSWERS on page 61.

SLICE TO MEET YOU

VIKING NAMES

DEADLY! CRAFTY VIKING NAME GENERATOR

1) Draw two circles on some card, one slightly bigger than the other, and cut them out.

2) Write some names from column A on the list opposite around the edge of the bigger circle.

3) Then write some names from column B on the list around the edge of the smaller circle.

You can do one for boys and one for girls or mix them up for even more mad names.

4) Join the two circles in the centre with a paper fastener.

5) Decorate with whatever Vikingy designs you like.

Now you've got yourself a Viking name generator! Close your eyes and turn the inner circle. Put your finger on the generator and then open your eyes! What's the first name you see? That's your Viking name!

BOYS		GIRLS	
A	B	A	B
BJÖRN	THE STOUT	ASTRID	THE BIG
OLAF	SKULL-SPLITTER	BRYNHILD	RED-CHEEK
SIGRID	THE RED	SIGRDIFA	THE FAIR
GORM	BLOODAXE	ALFDIS	DIRT-CHIN
ARVID	HAIRY BREECHES	SIV	THE CLUMSY
GUDRUN	LONG-NECK	TURID	SECOND-SIGHTED
EGIL	FOUL-FART	FREYA	MOSS-NECK
HELGI	FLAT-NOSE	GUDRUN	THE TALL
ULF	FORKBEARD	SOLVEIG	THE GREAT ONE
SVEN	TROLL-BURSTER	GRIMHILD	THIN-LEGGED
RAGNAR	ILL-LUCK	VIGDIS	THE HAUGHTY
ERIK	LEATHER-NECK	HILDUR	CRONE'S NOSE
ORM	THE BONELESS	SVANHILD	THE QUIET
NJALL	THE SQUINT-EYED	INGRID	THE ELEGANT
SIGURD	SLENDER-LEG	HALLGERD	SCATTERBRAIN
THORSTEN	THE STINGY	RANVEIG	TANGLE-HAIR
IVAR	BERSERK-KILLER	TORHILD	THE DEEP-MINDED

DEADLY! CRAFTY VIKING BROOCH

To Make the Brooch

Viking girls wore two matching brooches.

1) Cut an oval disc out of a thick sheet of card.

2) Glue string in whatever pattern you want to the disc. You can also drop blobs of glue to make circles.

3) Once glue is dry, place face down on a sheet of tin foil, leaving about a 2-cm edge that you can fold over the edges of the disc. Glue or tape the edges down.

RUB RUB

4) Turn the disc over and gently rub the foil over the string to make the pattern stand out.

5) Paint the raised string area in a contrasting colour – gold or bronze metallic paint.

GOLD

6) Tape a large safety pin to the back.

MAKE YOUR OWN BEADS

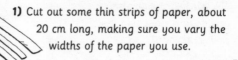

1) Cut out some thin strips of paper, about 20 cm long, making sure you vary the widths of the paper you use.

ROLL

2) Put some glue over one side of each strip, then roll them up tight.

3) When glue is dry, paint the beads nice bright colours.

4) Thread the beads on a piece of string or cotton and tie the ends to the safety pins behind the brooch, then attach to your apron.

THREAD

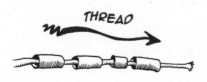

DEADLY! CRAFTY VIKING SHIELD

1) Take two sheets of thick cardboard and draw a circle on each of them of about 60 cm in diameter. You can make a circle this big by tying a pencil to one end of a piece of string and the other end to a nail. Put the nail in the centre of the cardboard and draw out the circle. Cut them both out.

2) To make the boss (the bumpy bit in the centre of the shield): cut a 2-litre plastic bottle in half and make six equal cuts to the bottom half.

3) Draw a hole around the bottom of the bottle in the centre of one of the pieces of cardboard. Don't make the hole too big!

4) Cut out the hole. Push the bottle bottom through the hole in one of the pieces of circular card and bend over the cut plastic bits then tape or glue them to the cardboard. Then glue the other piece of circular card over the top of that.

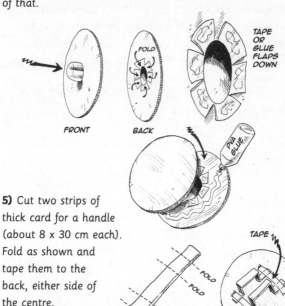

FRONT

BACK

TAPE OR GLUE FLAPS DOWN

FOLD

PVA GLUE

5) Cut two strips of thick card for a handle (about 8 x 30 cm each). Fold as shown and tape them to the back, either side of the centre.

FOLD
FOLD
FOLD
FOLD

TAPE

BACK

RED

YELLOW

SILVER

6) Paint the boss and the edge of the shield silver and the rest in the Viking style.

~~DEADLY!~~ ~~CRAFTY~~ VIKING HELMET

1) Cut out three strips of thick card. One measuring 65 x 3 cm and the other two measuring 40 x 3 cm. Take the longest one and wrap it round your head, just above your eyebrows. Glue the ends together. This is the headband.

GLUE

2) Mark the middles of the other two strips of card and glue together to form a cross shape.

3) Glue the ends of the cross shape inside the headband. GLUE GLUE GLUE

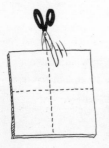

4) Take a sheet of card and cut out 4 pieces, 1.5 cm bigger than the spaces between the cross shape and the headband.

5) Glue the sheets into the inside of the helmet.

6) Insert paper fasteners into different points on the cross shape and headband. Use some tape to stick the ends down so they don't stick into your head, doofus!

7) Measure the space between your eyes. Draw two dots onto a sheet of card that distance apart, then draw eye-shaped holes around them.

8) Draw the rest of the eyepiece shape like the grey area here. Then cut out the eye-holes. Glue the eyepiece to the outside of the headband. You can draw fierce 'eyebrows' on the eyepiece if you want.

9) Paint the whole lot with silver paint. Voilà! Your own Viking helmet. (Just don't try stopping an axe blow with it though!)

45

EAT LIKE A VIKING!
NÄSSELSOPPA – OR NETTLE SOUP!

Serves 4

½ carrier bag of fresh nettle leaves, chopped (Don't forget to wear gloves when you're picking them, ya eejit!)

Chives, chopped

3 tbsp plain flour

1.5 litres (6 cups) of water

2 chicken or vegetable stock cubes (Vikings would have made their own stock)

2 hardboiled eggs

2 tbsp butter

salt and pepper

1) Rinse the nettle leaves in cold water to get rid of any creepy-crawlies – though you could leave those in for extra *crunch*!

2) Melt the butter, add the flour and stir. When golden, add the water, stock cubes, nettles and chives and boil for about 10 minutes.

3) Season with a little salt and pepper. Serve with half a boiled egg per portion.

Don't worry about this soup making you feel *prickly* – it's perfectly safe to eat!

This is Brynhild Truth-Twister. She spins yarns as much as she weaves wool! Which of her statements do you think are true? **Answers below.**

A) VIKING WOMEN WORK FOR 14 HOURS OR LONGER EVERY DAY.

B) VIKING CHILDREN GO TO SCHOOL.

C) VIKING MEN AND WOMEN MARRY FOR LOVE.

D) VIKING WOMEN CAN'T GET DIVORCED FROM THEIR HUSBANDS.

E) VIKING PEOPLE ARE REALLY DIRTY AND SMELLY.

ANSWERS: Brynhild is such a liar! She managed to tell the truth only once! a) True – Viking women worked very hard preparing food, cooking, weaving, brewing, sewing, cleaning, spinning, baking AND she did her husband's jobs when he was away. b) Nope, no school! HOORAY! Viking kids stayed home all day, but BOO! They had loads of chores to do. c) Afraid not. Most Viking marriages were arranged by the marrying families. Fathers of the bride got a 'bride-price' from the groom. d) Untrue. They could divorce a man who was cruel by stating it in front of witnesses. e) False!

FISHAMBLE STREET

A VIKING (SOAP) OPERA

Archaeologists found tons of stuff when the Wood Quay area of Dublin was dug up by builders. Most of it ended up in the National Museum in Dublin. See if you can find these things in this episode of Fishamble Street. Good luck finding them all! **Answers on page 62**.

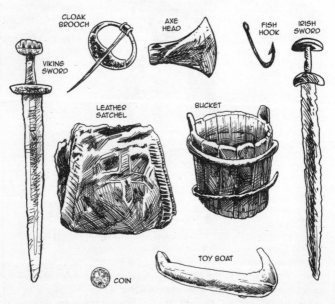

CLOAK BROOCH

AXE HEAD

FISH HOOK

IRISH SWORD

VIKING SWORD

LEATHER SATCHEL

BUCKET

TOY BOAT

COIN

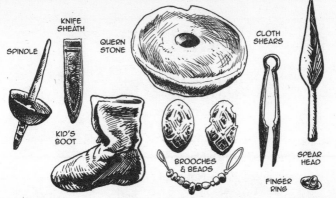

49

50

51

52

MISTER ULF! MISTER ULF! YOUR FISHING BOAT'S BEEN STOLEN!

WHAT?!? OH NO! I'D BETTER GET DOWN TO THE QUAY RIGHT AWAY!

HEE HEE! ORM'S A GENIUS!

AT ORM AND GRIMHILD'S HOUSE, ORM IS 'FIXING' THE LOOM—

... AND I DON'T KNOW WHY YOU HANG AROUND WITH THAT FAT, UGLY, LAZY LUMP ULF!

ULF'S NOT LAZY!

TAP TAP

MISTER ORM! MISTER ORM! YOUR BOAT'S BEEN STOLEN!

GREAT! I MEAN, 'AWWW'! BETTER GO, DEAR!

THAT WORKED A TREAT, ORM!

SLAP!

WOO-HOO! NOW FOR A GREAT NIGHT OUT, ULF!

53

DOWN AT THE QUAY, KING SITRIC'S MEN BRAVELY GUARD THE CITY--

YAWN! THIS IS SO *BORING*!

EVERYBODY ELSE IS IN THE MEAD HALL HAVING *FUN*! IT'S NOT *FAIR*!

THE IRISH AREN'T GONNA INVADE TONIGHT! C'MON, LET'S GO!

JUST AS WELL I CAME DOWN ...

GOODY!

... 'COS IT LOOKS LIKE THE IRISH *ARE* GONNA INVADE TONIGHT!

HEH HEH!

... AND WATERFORD IS *SO* CLEAN AND *SO* FRIENDLY.

ER – WHY DON'T WE GO TO THE MEAD HALL? I HEARD THERE'S A GREAT *SKALD* ON LATER!

YUSS.

55

56

HEY – ISN'T THAT ULF AND ORM'S BOAT?!

I THOUGHT IT WAS SUPPOSED TO BE *STOLEN!*

THE VALKYRIE

I SMELL SOMETHING *FISHY!*

BACK AT THE FORTRESS—

I MAY HAVE LOST MY BOOT IN THE MUD ...

... BUT I *SAVED* DUBLIN!

HELLO, OLAF.

IN THE MEAD HALL—

SIGURD THE SKALD IS ABOUT TO BEGIN, ULF! *SKOL!*

SKOL! WE FOOLED EVERYONE, ORM!

GOOD EVENING, LADIES AND GENTLEVIKINGS!

HA HA HA HA

I JUST ROWED IN FROM NORWAY AND NOW MY ARMS ARE REALLY *THOR!*

57

DID YOU FIND
ALL THE OBJECTS
FROM THE MUSEUM?
ANSWERS ON
PAGE 62.

NEXT TIME ON

ULF AND ORM
FALL OUT OVER
A BURIED TREASURE
HOARD AND OLAF
MEETS A GIRL.

TIMELINE

795 – The first recorded Viking attacks occur on monasteries on Rechru Island, Inishmurray and Inishbofin.

798–807 – Having figured out monasteries were full of unprotected gold – and Vikings love their bling – Viking raids start happening more often.

811–12 – The Irish strike back when the warriors of Ulaid in the north-east defeat a band of Viking raiders. Then the men of Umall, Co. Mayo and the King of Eóganacht Locha Léin in the south-west slaughter a load of Vikings.

824 – Vikings raid Skellig Michael off the south-west coast and capture the abbot called Étgal for a ransom. When nobody pays up, they starve him to death.

825 – Again, the Ulaid defeat the Vikings.

835 – The Irish defeat Vikings at Derry.

836 – Starting to get cheeky now, the first inland (not on the coast) raid by the Vikings takes place on the lands of the southern Uí Néill (Co. Meath), where they kill loads of people and take lots of captives. Also, they raid Connacht in the west.

837 – Having decided they rather like Ireland, hordes of Vikings arrive in sixty ships and this time they go further inland up the Rivers Liffey and Boyne. They plunder farms, churches and fortresses.

840–41 – Vikings spend the whole winter on Lough Neagh.

841–42 – Vikings start building fortified bases called *longphuirt* around the country and stay the winter in Dublin. The first Irish-Viking alliance is formed.

845 – The High King of Ireland captures and drowns a Viking leader called Thorgest. The Vikings capture the abbot of Armagh called Forannán but he returns home the following year.

848–9 – Utterly sick of their carry-on, the Irish start winning loads of battles against the Vikings.

851–852 – Danish Vikings arrive and attack the Norwegian Vikings, wanting to take control of Dublin. They fight a massive sea battle in Carlingford Lough.

902 – Irish clans seize Dublin. Vikings flee to Britain.

917 – Vikings return to Dublin and take it back.

928 – Viking massacre at Dunmore Cave, Kilkenny.

936 – Irish burn Dublin down but the Vikings quickly build it up again.

976–978 – Brian Boru becomes king of the Dal gCais, defeats Vikings and takes Limerick. Then becomes King of Munster.

980 – High King Máel Sechnaill seizes Dublin then the Vikings take it back.

997 – Brian and Máel agree to divide Ireland equally between them – Brian as King of the South (except Dublin), and Máel as King of the North.

999–1001 – Brian breaks the agreement. Abandoned by his allies, Máel submits to Brian.

1001–1013 – Brian expands his territories and becomes King of Ireland (except Dublin) in 1002. Ireland is quite peaceful for a while. But Brian has stepped on lots of toes on his way to the top and his enemies wait for a chance to take him down, especially Máel Morda, King of Leinster. (Is *everyone* called Máel?!)

1014 – Nothing of interest happens this year. Oh wait! Just the Battle of Clontarf in April! BB and Máel Morda are killed and Máel Sechnaill takes over as High King. Viking power in Ireland is greatly reduced.

1014–1042 – Sitric Silkbeard stays on as King of Dublin until 1036. He dies in exile four years later. The Vikings integrate completely with the Irish, becoming Christians and generally behaving themselves.

1169 – The Norman Invasion of Ireland (not an invasion by people called Norman, no) begins, but that's another story ...

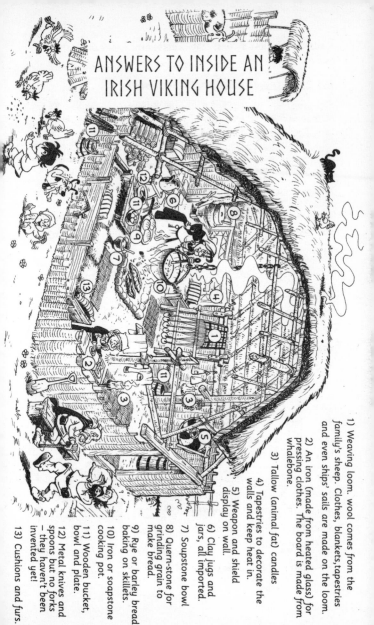

1) Weaving loom. wool comes from the family's sheep. Clothes, blankets, tapestries and even ships' sails are made on the loom.

2) An iron (made from heated glass) for pressing clothes. The board is made from whalebone.

3) Tallow (animal fat) candles

4) Tapestries to decorate the walls and keep heat in.

5) Weapon and shield display on wall.

6) Clay jugs and jars, all imported.

7) Soapstone bowl

8) Quern-stone for grinding grain to make bread.

9) Rye or barley bread baking on skillets.

10) Iron or soapstone cooking pot.

11) Wooden bucket, bowl and plate.

12) Metal knives and spoons but no forks – they haven't been invented yet!

13) Cushions and furs.

ANSWERS TO FISHAMBLE STREET

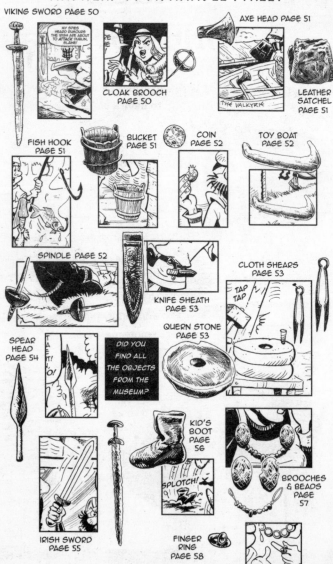

VIKING SWORD PAGE 50

CLOAK BROOCH PAGE 50

AXE HEAD PAGE 51

LEATHER SATCHEL PAGE 51

THE VALKYRIE

FISH HOOK PAGE 51

BUCKET PAGE 51

COIN PAGE 52

TOY BOAT PAGE 52

SPINDLE PAGE 52

KNIFE SHEATH PAGE 53

CLOTH SHEARS PAGE 53

TAP TAP

SPEAR HEAD PAGE 54

DID YOU FIND ALL THE OBJECTS FROM THE MUSEUM?

QUERN STONE PAGE 53

KID'S BOOT PAGE 56

SPLOTCH!

BROOCHES & BEADS PAGE 57

IRISH SWORD PAGE 55

FINGER RING PAGE 58

Happy
World Book Day!

As a charity, our mission is to encourage every child and young person to enjoy reading, and to have a book of their own.

Everyone is a reader — that includes you!

Whether you enjoy **comics**, **fact books**, **adventure stories**, **recipes** – books are for everyone and every book counts.

On **World Book Day**, everyone comes together to have **FUN** reading. Talking about and sharing books with your friends and family makes reading even more memorable and magic.

Illustration by Allen Fatimaharan © 2021

LÁ DOMHANDA NA LEABHAR
WORLD **BOOK DAY**
3 MARCH 2022

Where will your **reading journey** take you next?

1 **Take a trip to your local bookshop**
Brimming with brilliant books and helpful booksellers to share awesome reading recommendations, bookshops are magical places. You can even enjoy booky events and meet your favourite authors and illustrators!

Find your nearest bookseller at booksaremybag.com/Home

2 **Join your local library**
A world awaits you in your local library – that place where all the books you could ever want to read awaits. Even better, you can borrow them for **FREE**! Libraries can offer expert advice on what to read next, as well as free family reading events.

Find your local library at librariesireland.ie/find-your-local-library

Scan here to visit our website!

3 **Check out the World Book Day website**
Looking for reading tips, advice and inspiration? There is so much to discover at worldbookday.com/getreading, packed with book recommendations, fun activities, audiobooks, and videos to enjoy on your own or as a family, as well as competitions and all the latest book news galore.

NATIONAL BOOK tokens